Why Network Marketing is the Best Home Based Business You Should be Doing

Fast Track Your Way to Success

InfluencerNetworker.net

Discover the best LEVERAGE SYSTEM that can generate you more and more money even When you are Gone

By

Anthony Langmartey

(Entrepreneur, Network Marketer, Author & Pastor)

Author's Note

This book is designed to provide competent and reliable information regarding the subject matter covered. However, it is sold with the understanding that the author is not engaged in rendering legal, financial or other professional advice. The author specifically disclaims any liability that is incurred from the use or application of the contents of this book.

Copyright

Dedication

I dedicate this book to my lovely mother Elizabeth Mamle Tettey for her unfading effort of my upbringing in the light of the Creator and to you my cherished reader for your keenness in search of financial freedom and independence.

TABLE OF CONTENTS

Introduction

Opportunities Are Not Seen By the Blind

People of vision see the front side of opportunities while people without vision only see the backside. — Dr. Mike Ike

Opportunities are only seen and grabbed by those who have the ability to see beyond the human eye.

The 1993/4 academic year was disrupted by a general strike of the Academic Staff Union of Nigerian Universities That was during the dictatorship of the late General Sani Abacha. The strike continued for days, which turned into weeks and months. General Abacha refused to pay the striking workers for almost a year. There was this professor of mathematics who could no longer cater for his family due to the strike. One day his wife said to him, "Professor Thomas", (calling him by his name for the first time in 20 years of marriage, instead of the usual honey or darling.) "There is no food in this house, the children are out of school and you parade yourself as a professor." The professor answered, "but you know that they are not paying us, you know that very well, so what do you want me to do, kill myself for you, tell me?" The wife retorted, "So if they don't call you people back again, you won't find something else to do, please use your professorship brains and get us food in this house. Professor, do something now, fast, before it's too late".

When You Are Hungry You Will Think

For the first time, Mr. Professor sat down to think of alternatives (there are always alternatives). He was living in a big house with a large compound in the teachers' quarters. An idea occurred to him; he constructed a birdhouse and bought some day old chicks. In three months' time, he sold them, bought more and more and gradually he owns a big poultry farm. He now makes 5 times what they pay him as a Professor from his poultry business. *"A wise man creates more opportunities than he finds"* — Beacon.

You see, the opportunity was there but the Professor couldn't see it until challenges made him. Now he is much richer than he was and is assured from a lucrative business after retirement from his professional career.

You can conspicuously see the veracity of General MacArthur's statement, *"There is no security on his planet, there is only opportunity."* Instead of looking for security, look for an opportunity. No job is forever secure. Even mega companies are laying off workers and you're not sure of future events that may affect your job.

You succeed by utilizing the opportunity and making the most of them. Sometimes, your breakthrough may not be in your chosen career, *but in an opportunity that you may underestimate at first sight.*

Unlimited Opportunities Awaits You, Grab Them Before They Expire

There are numerous opportunities awaiting you. No matter what you do or where you live, there are still many untapped opportunities. The fact is that opportunities are always there. They will never cease. They come and they go. The Bible says, **"While the earth remains... opportunities shall never cease" (Genesis 8:22, paraphrased).**

Many people think that they must travel to other countries before they can prosper. The truth is that changing your geographical location is not the remedy, a paradigm shift is inevitable. This is why many people travel abroad and haven't succeeded but others come back home and experience mega breakthroughs.

Many researchers have over the years delved into discovering why some people are more successful than others. Countless numbers of people from all walks of life have been interviewed in the quest to identify the common denominators of success. Almost all of them have expressed the importance of opportunity maximization.

Life and destiny can be instantly transformed by a single opportunity.

Successful people are people who can easily recognize opportunities and grab them. *If you are ever going to move ahead, you must see fast, hear fast, and act fast.* Many people can't see new opportunities; others see but refuse to act while others act when it is too late, only very few see and grab opportunities.

Some of the available opportunities do not need 21 days of fasting and prayers or deliverance to see them. It demands trying new things and acting immediately. Ellen Metcalf said, *"You have to recognize when the right place and the right time fuse and take advantage of that opportunity. There are plenty of opportunities out there, you can't sit back and watch."*

There is no time to waste, opportunities are to be grabbed immediately they are spotted before they expire because opportunities don't last forever. They come and they go. Publilius Syrus said, *"While we stop to think, we often miss our opportunity"*

Sometimes when you see an opportunity, you need to loan or borrow or dispose of what you have in order to grab the opportunity. Remember that opportunities don't last forever, they come and go, and other ones emerge and also go.

Many opportunities demand that you act fast. Delay is dangerous in many cases. The Holy Bible also admits it. The Bible says, ***"Again, the kingdom of heaven is like unto treasure hid in a field; the which when a man hath found, he hideth, and for joy thereof goeth and selleth all that he hath, and buyeth that field" (Matthew 13:44 KJV).***

You can sell what you have in order to grab an opportunity, however, be careful and research the risk meticulously so it won't backfire.

Fortunate for the Eyes that See and the Ears that Hears

"Learn to listen. Opportunities could be knocking at your door very softly"

— *Frank Tyger* —

Success is for those who have eyes that can see opportunities. Opportunities abound, it only takes seeing eyes and hearing ears. Many people have eyes but they don't see. Take notice of this Scripture: *"Then the king of Syria warred against Israel, and took counsel with his servants, saying, in such and such a place shall be my camp. And the man of God sent unto the king of Israel, saying, Beware that thou pass not such a place; for thither the Syrians are come down. And the king of Israel sent to the place which the man of God told him and warned him of, and saved himself there, not once nor twice. Therefore the heart of the king of Syria was sore troubled for this thing; and he called his servants, and said unto them, will ye not shew me which of us is for the king of Israel? And one of his servants said, none, my lord, O king: but Elisha, the prophet that is in Israel, telleth the king of Israel the words that thou speakest in thy bedchamber. And he said, Go and spy where he is, that I may send and fetch him. And it was told him, saying, Behold, he is in Dothan. And when the servant of the man of God was risen early, and gone forth, behold, a host compassed the city both with horses and chariots. And his servant said unto him, Alas, my master! how shall we do? And he answered, Fear not: for they that be with us are more than they that be with them. And Elisha prayed, and said, LORD, I pray thee, open his eyes, that he may see. And the LORD opened the eyes of the young man; and he saw: and, behold, the mountain was full of horses and chariots of fire round about Elisha"* (2 *Kings 6:8-13, 15-17 KJV*).

The young man Gehazi was never blind; he had eyes which he used in seeing the Syrian army that has surrounded them. Unfortunately, he could not see God's provision. He couldn't see available opportunities. Think of this, whether he saw the chariots of fire, the angels and the horses or not they were still there. That's how it is, whether you see opportunities or not they are there. It took the prayers of the prophet Elisha for his eyes to be opened to see the provision of God.

There are uncountable opportunities around you only that you can't see them. If you can't see them, you can't utilize them and others will take advantage of them. That is why when you are crying that things are bad, others are rejoicing that things are improving because they see what you don't see.

I remembered when I was a teen, I was going somewhere with three of my friends, they stepped on a GHS 50 ($10) note on the path without seeing it, I then picked it. The same way, you have been stepping on wonderful opportunities, without recognizing it.

Learn to move with the changing times and opportunities. When it gets cold nobody tells you to cover yourself. When it is hot your reaction changes. Look around for the things that are on board and move with it.

Every circumstance, problem, hardship, disappointment, government, etc., has its own in-built opportunities for success. A positive attitude will help you discover the opportunities, but a negative attitude will keep you critical and unprogressive.

In this book, I'm going to show you why network marketing is the best home-based business you should get yourself involved to achieve financial freedom. This isn't just about changing the type of business you're working with; it's about knowing what is working and reliable. Note that for you to be successful in life, you have to get access to the right information and this is what this book provides.

Welcome to the business of the 21st century and beyond.

CHAPTER 1

WHAT IS NETWORK MARKETING?

"The greatest opportunity in the world is network marketing"

— John Kalench —

Network Marketing is a business model in which a distributor *network* is needed to build the business. Usually, such businesses are also *multi-level marketing* in nature in that payouts occur at more than one level.

Types of Network Marketing Companies

There are two main types of network marketing companies. They are:

1. The service-based network marketing companies

These are companies that provide services rather than products.

2. The product-based network marketing companies

These companies are also called multi-level marketing companies (MLM). Product-Based network marketing companies utilize the synergy principle effectively. These are also known as direct sales companies — companies that sell products to consumers through independent distributors.

In my opinion, product-based network marketing is the best as compared to service-based network marketing to build a solid and true residual income.

As to service-based network marketing, although it might be easier it's not necessarily more profitable... which means you can be capped at how much volume you could accumulate per customer in your team.

Network marketing companies allow you to build your own business under a parent company — they provide you a platform to build your business empire. It takes a lot to establish your own company and to avoid that you can operate under a network company.

The channel of distribution is from the company to independent distributors, then to the consumers.

The advantage is that you as a partner of the company have access to the company's products and you as a distributor or partner or an affiliate is the only means or channel through which consumers can get the company's products.

You buy the products at a wholesale price from your network marketing company and then sell them to your consumers at a retail price. Because you are a partner of the company, the company even pays you a 50% commission for buying the products at a wholesale price from them.

And you also earn additional profits by giving the products to your consumers at a retail price. In this way, you earn double money whenever you move the company's products to consumers.

Non-network marketing companies do not offer this opportunity. Non-network marketing companies will never give any amount of money to any person just by buying products from them at a wholesale price. An only product -based network marketing companies do that.

Network marketing companies generally do no advert on radio, television, newspaper, or any form of the media advertising platform, the money that would have been spent on such media advertising platforms is thereby paid back to you (a partner of the company) as bonuses.

Success in network marketing is *based on teamwork*. Teamwork means that we share a common ideal, embrace a common goal, regardless of our differences; we strive shoulder to shoulder, confidence in one another's faith, trust, and commitment.

In the end, teamwork can be summed up in five short words... *we believe in each other.*

Product-based network marketing companies also use the power of duplication and multiplication.

The Power of Duplication and Multiplication

"The law of multiplication is the eighth wonder of the world"

— Walter Chrysler —

Network marketing success comes as a result of duplication and multiplication — without them, there wouldn't be a network marketing success.

To create wealth and achieve success, you must learn and use the opportunity offered by the principle of duplication and multiplication.

This is the opportunity to share what you do with others and thereby duplicate yourself in others — creating a thousand of yourself.

You must learn how to develop your business to the point that without your presence, the business goes on and you still make money.

Network marketing companies allow you to introduce or refer other people to the business and they, in turn, also introduce or refer others thereby creating a team of distributors or partners.

The compensation plan is structured in such a way that you are paid a certain percentage of your downlines' purchase and/or recruits.

Downlines here simply means those that you have recruited and connected to your network marketing business — your team.

The duplication and multiplication principle can be *maxed* in this way. As soon as you partner with a network marketing company, the first thing to do is to introduce or refer three people and these three downlines should also recruit three people each and the three people should also recruit three other people each and so on and so forth.

So the law of multiplication is also the power of duplication. An example of the law of multiplication is 3x3x3x3x3x3x3 = 2187

Let's break it down:

(3x3 = **9**), (9x3 = **27**), (27x3 = **81**), (81x3 = **243**), (243x3 = **729**), (729x3 = **2187**)

By your effort of bringing 3 people into your network marketing business, and by the power of duplication in just 6 multiple times, you now have 2,187 downlines or partners helping you to achieve success.

You will be paid on all the activities of these people. With this principle, tremendous wealth can be created. And as a result, you will retire young and retire rich.

Network marketing is the way of the rich. To be rich is simple, *do what the rich do and you too will be rich.* It gives you the opportunity to make residual income as opposed to linear income.

CHAPTER 2
TYPES OF INCOME

There are 2 types of income. They are:

1. Ordinary or Linear Income

2. Passive or Residual Income

Let's learn something about these two different types of income.

Linear Income Vs Residual Income

Ordinary/Linear Income

It is the income you make as a result of your personal investment of time and energy or the work you do. Examples of linear income are salaries, contracts, wages, and stipends.

Research has shown that you cannot be wealthy as a result of your personal effort alone; you need a system that allows you to make money through the effort of others and that is network marketing.

Passive/Residual Income

Have you ever used one of those spring-loaded water faucets that some public restrooms install to save water? When you turn the water on, you have to hold the faucet there, because when you let go, it bounces back to the off position.

Most people's income source (ordinary income) works just like that faucet: You get a little money flowing, and then when you let go, it bounces back to off. You can never build freedom that way. What you want is a money faucet that you can let go of once you've turned it on, *because it stays on by itself.*

It's not just about having income today, tomorrow, and next week; it's about securing your income in perpetuity.

This is *passive income*, also known as *residual income*: income that continues coming in, over and over, long after the effort and capital it took to create the source of the income.

Shifting yourself into the Big Business Quadrant is a strong step in that direction, but not all businesses will create passive income. If you own a restaurant, you earn income only when you prepare and sell a meal.

If your business fixes air conditioners, you earn income only when you provide that service. Even high-salaried doctors and lawyer earn money only when they see patients or clients.

If no patients or clients require their knowledge and services in a particular week, the income faucet springs shut again and there's no money coming in that week.

According to Robert Kiyosaki, *"What most people need is an AVENUE to create passive income. Knowing this, Donald Trump and I teamed up to evaluate the many kinds of business structures that can create passive income and published our results in a book, We Want You to Be Rich. So what did we discover? We found that one business model stood out from the rest. This particular business model creates passive income, but requires relatively little cash investment to start up. It has very low overhead and can be operated on a flexible part-time basis until it generates enough cash flow for the entrepreneur to transition out of his current full-time job. That business model is called* **network marketing.**"

In sum, residual income is the income you make whether you are personally involved or not. Income from shares, equity, stocks and bonds, real estate, network marketing, etc. are known to be residual income.

You must have a system that pays you money without your personal involvement or pays for the work you did not do, or for the work you did once but you continue to receive from it.

So what is that system? It's simply "Network Marketing", period.

CHAPTER 3

WHAT DO THE STATISTICS SAY?

According to the Direct Selling Association, *"it is estimated that about 15.6 million people in the U.S.A are involved in network marketing and in a total of 92 million worldwide."*

Traditional Marketing versus Network Marketing

Traditional Business Marketing Model

VS

Network Marketing Business Model

A traditional company would typically have a Vice President of Marketing with several regional managers reporting directly to them. Those regional managers would recruit, hire, train and manage several area managers who, in turn, would each recruit, hire, train and manage several sales representatives.

The sales representatives are then responsible for selling the company's products or services.

Plotted on a piece of paper, the shape of the traditional organization would look like a triangle or pyramid.

It's quite obvious that the higher the level the higher the pay and that there is less room at the top for advancement.

It is also evident that it is mathematically impossible for each and every sales representative or employee to rise to the top regardless of how good a job they do!

Here is the difference.

First and foremost, Network Marketing is different. Each individual starts at exactly the same level – at the top of their own organization, has exactly the same opportunity as everyone else and is compensated in direct proportion to the activity or success that they have had an influence in generating.

Secondly, one doesn't need to be a salesperson to reap the level of financial benefits normally associated with company owners, sales managers, and marketers.

Thirdly, in Network Marketing, we work with, when and for whom we choose.

And last but not least, different than in a traditional company, we only work for ourselves and those whose activity generates income for us!

We may also choose to work with those which we are generating income for, because, in most cases, they don't make money unless we do.

What Are People Saying About Network Marketing?

Network marketing business model is powerful because *it works*—and I'm not the only person saying so, either.

Tom Peters, the legendary management expert and author of the classic best-seller *In Search of Excellence*, describes network marketing as *"the first truly revolutionary shift in marketing since the advent of 'modern' marketing at Procter and Gamble and Harvard Business School over fifty years ago."*

The emerging success of network marketing has been written about in such journals as *Forbes, Fortune, Newsweek, TIME, U.S.A. News & World Report, U.S.A. Today, The New York Times*, and *The Wall Street Journal*. Fifteen years ago, you couldn't have gotten a single one of these journals to give this business the time of day. Now, look at what a recent issue of *Fortune* said about network marketing: *"An investor's dream ... the best-kept secret of the business world ... an industry with steady annual growth, healthy cash flows, high return on invested capital, and long-term prospects for global expansion."*

Warren Buffett and Richard Branson couldn't be more different. Buffett drives a pickup and lives in Omaha; Branson flies his own airline and lives on his own island in the British Virgin Islands. But they have three things in common. They are both billionaires. They are both extremely practical men. And they have both owned network marketing companies.

Does that tell you something?

Citigroup, Jockey, L'Oréal, Mars, Remington, and Unilever: Guess what they all have in common? They've all put a toe in the network marketing water—in some cases, right up to their hips.

Today, network marketing is recognized by many experts and accomplished businesspeople as one of the fastest-growing business models in the world.

While traditional jobs are difficult to find, a home-based business using network marketing skills is an easy stand-by option.

It offers people the chance to earn a fair income representing goods or services that they love while being able to pay the bills and spend more time with their families.

For those that need a little extra cash to make ends meet, just a few hours a week with a home-based network marketing business can create the extra income that is needed.

What does Statistics say?

Statistic #1: There are 38 million home-based businesses in the United States

A home -based network marketing business is common and easy to start than before and the support systems are in abundance, the training is better and the community is bigger than it has ever been before.

For instance, if you want to be a self-employed person or start a small scale or sole proprietorship business, you have to rent a building, buy inventory, advertise your product or service, and hopefully, make some money.

The facts will tell you that you stand a 50% chance of going out of business in your 1st year and a 90% chance of going out of business by your 5th year.

While that may also be true for a home-based network marketing business, the advantage lies in the *lower liability*. With a home-based network marketing business, you can run the business off a laptop from your home or anywhere in the world.

There's no need to sign a long-term lease on a retail building and you don't have to purchase business insurance. You also don't have to spend large sums of money on advertising. Factually, the liability is *lower*.

When running a home-based network marketing business, keep in mind that *it is a must to leverage technology as much as possible. You have to build an online brand and also have to reach out to people in a friendly and non-spammy way. Ultimately, you have to train your team on their time.*

Statistic #2: Other true facts

1. Someone starts a home-based network marketing business every 10 seconds in the world today.

2. Networking marketing businesses that are based out of a home have an 80% greater chance of success than other traditional small businesses.

3. About 38 million people work at least part-time out of their home using network marketing industry-based skills every day.

4. The average bonus check a home-based networking marketing representative receives every month is greater than $500.

5. By 2020, it is estimated that 75% of American households will be operating a home-based network marketing business at least part-time.

6. The average worker in this industry who works full-time as a network marketer earns more than $75,000 per year

7. 1 out of every 5 home-based network marketing businesses grosses at least 6 figures in sales annually.

8. More than half a million people will create a home-based business using network marketing industry skills in 2020 alone.

9. More than 15 million people currently work full time at home in a network marketing business.

A Short History of Network Marketing

It is a generally accepted history that the first multi-level marketing plan was introduced in 1945 by the California Vitamin Company.

1n 1949, two young men named Rich DeVos and Jay VanAndel became Nutrilite distributors. In the ensuing decade, they build a large, prosperous organization across America.

What's More to Network Marketing?

Network marketing or Multi-Level Marketing is basically a method of moving products or services from the manufacturer to the end consumer without the middle man through the most powerful method of advertisement — "word of mouth."

The Federal Trade Commission (FTC) warns "Not all multi-level marketing plans are legitimate. Some are pyramid schemes. It's best not to get involved in plans where the money you make is based primarily on the number of distributors you recruit and your sales to them."

Multi-Level Marketing pays based on performance standards. If you perform to a certain standard, you earn whatever that standard or level pays.

Unlike traditional direct selling, this was an ongoing payment whenever the customer re-ordered: allowing direct sellers to build a sales organization that could generate a residual like income.

Independent distributors of network marketing companies develop their organizations by either building an active customer base, who buy direct from the company, or by recruiting a downline of independent distributors who also build a customer base, thereby expanding the overall organization.

Today, Network Marketing is reported to be a $100 billion industry, internationally, made up of FORTUNE 500 and New York Stock Exchange companies.

Most experts advise that before joining any network marketing company, the company should be registered by the Direct Sales Administration.

The U.S 2010 statistic showed a $28.56 billion in Direct Sales (Network Marketing)

Currently, more than 15.8 Million people are working from home full-time.

Do you still need more facts and real statistics about the home-based network marketing industry? Well, contact me and I will give you the link to download the free report from Art Jonak, the Mastermind Event Founder.

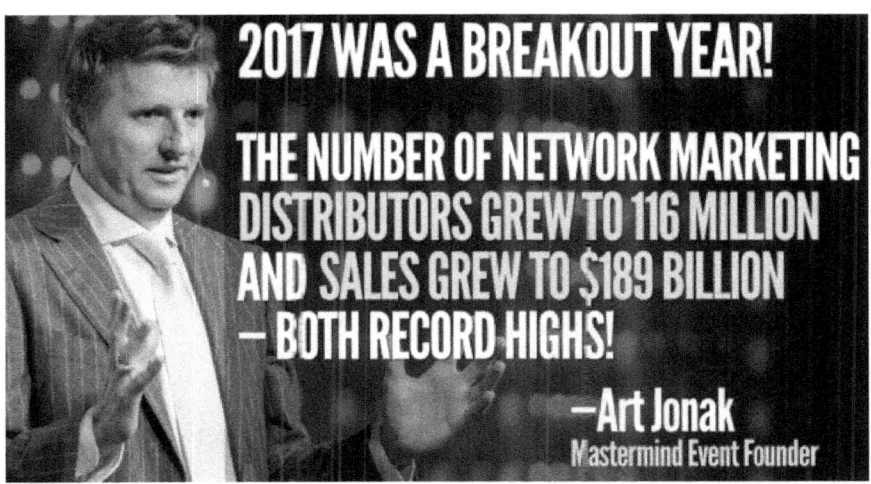

Network marketing is the business of the 21st Century and beyond.

CHAPTER 4

ADVANTAGES OF NETWORK MARKETING

"I would rather earn 1% of 100 people's effort than 100% of my own efforts"

— *John D. Rockefeller* —

As you build a strong team through a network marketing company, you will marvel at so many good things that can happen to you. Some of the advantages and benefits you will enjoy are as follows:

1. Quality products: Network marketing companies thrives on high-quality products. Being a distributor or partner gives you access to the products at a wholesale price which the public or non-partners of the company do not. You can always trust the products.

Products are the bloodline of network marketing companies; therefore, network marketing companies put a lot of money into the research and production of quality products.

2. Time and effort: The principle of time leverage is what makes Network marketing stick. You share what you do with other people and you get paid for whatever business they generate — that is leveraging on other people's time and effort.

For instance, if you invest 7 hours every week to your network marketing business and share the opportunity with three people who also invest 7 hours each making a total of 21 hours per week.

It means that you will be paid a proportion of what is generated in those 21 hours.

However, it must be noted that in the network marketing business, at first, most of your effort and time is not adequately rewarded, but as your team grows, *you get paid for the work you did not do.* At this time, you will have enough time for yourself and your family while you still earn more money.

3. Unlimited income potential: Network marketing gives you access to unlimited income potential through the duplication principle. As your team grows, your income grows accordingly. You have the opportunity to decide how much you receive monthly and this is opposed to a job situation whereby you receive an agreed or fixed amount.

4. Recognition: In network marketing, your effort and every position you achieve is recognized. Recognition is the trademark of network marketing companies. In most cases, gold, silver and bronze medals are awarded.

5. International business opportunity: Most network marketing companies are international. The compensation plan allows you to register or recruit people outside your country and you are rewarded from their activities. In this way, you can be in one country and earn money from many countries, just by registering people in those countries. Through this opportunity, one can build a strong network marketing business around the world using the internet.

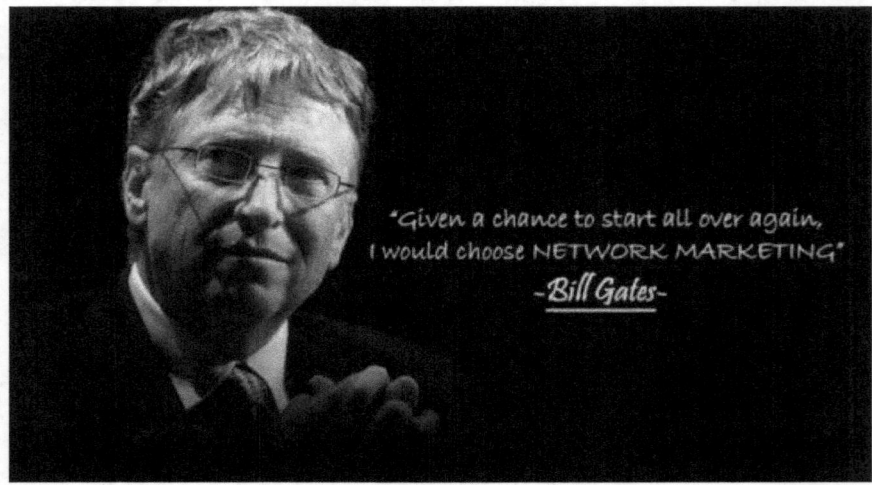

"Given a chance to start all over again, I would choose NETWORK MARKETING" -Bill Gates-

6. Incentives: Network marketing companies give incentives to their distributors or partners. Such incentives come in the form of cars, luxury house and holidays abroad (all expenses paid by the company) and university scholarships. All these and many more are made available to you.

7. No special qualification or literacy: To become a partner or distributor of a network marketing company does not require certain qualification or literacy. You can be an illiterate, a literate, a graduate, a rich or poor person, young or old, as long as you work smart and hard, you will be rewarded.

8. Making New Friends: You make new business friends both locally and internationally from network marketing.

9. You acquire important skills: Network marketing gives you the opportunity to learn vital skills such as communication and leadership skills and at the same time earn residual income while practicing. You *learn practically* not theoretically.

10. Willable: After building a strong network business, you can will it to anybody in most network marketing companies.

11. Does not require employees, debt and complicated administrative procedures

Rather than having several employees working with other employees under one roof for the benefit of someone else's company, with Network Marketing, we have a bunch of home-based business owners, working under their own roof, networking with other home-based business owners, all working for their own companies.

This concept provides an incentive and opportunity of multiplication and duplication for each home-based business owner equal to or greater than that of the owners of traditional businesses with multiple employees and locations, without all the hassles associated with traditional businesses!

It requires no debt, no employees and no complicated administrative procedures. With Network Marketing, we work with and for other people and other people work with and for us.

12. Eliminates taking orders, doing deliveries, keeping track of people, paying people and international borders

When you purchase a product or service, usually over 50% of the retail cost is associated with marketing! That would be any cost associated with getting someone to buy the product plus any cost incurred once it is produced by the factory.

With Network Marketing, the products are shipped directly to the consumer from the factory.

Those monies normally associated with marketing are paid to several home-based Network Marketing businesses owners which had previous network marketing or internet marketing influence in the referral of the customer!

13. Getting a 50% commission of wholesale products

One exciting thing is that most network marketing companies thrive on high-quality products.

Many customers will not buy inferior products and there is limited benefit to paying a little less for a product on the short run.

When you buy a product from your network marketing company to use or sell, you buy it at a wholesale price, and in return, the company pays you a 50% commission or rebate.

In effect, you've saved 50% on the products you purchased. That may save you a few dollars. Although saving money is important, the concept of earning money on products that we are already buying is far more exciting.

14. Earning a Residual income as opposed to Linear or ordinary income

Imagine having a network of thousands of customers purchasing quality products or services each month where you receive a few dollars per month for each customer!

Remember, these are products or services that we are all already buying, or should be, and this is money that is normally paid to others.

In essence, the simple process of referring to other customers who also refer other customers to a Network Marketing company presents an opportunity for a redistribution of the wealth to you and me, the consumer!

CHAPTER 5

HOW DOES A HOME-BASED NETWORK MARKETING BUSINESS WORKS?

In Network Marketing, there are customers and also independent representatives who operate as a home-based business. The customers may also be independent representatives.

Independent representatives can earn management positions if they so desire. Different than in traditional business, each independent representative is given the opportunity and responsibility of both recruiting customers and other independent representatives.

Each independent representative is owner, president, and vice-president of marketing for their own home-based network marketing business.

Network Marketing is a word of mouth business. By spreading the word, the network marketing marketer identifies others who desire to be customers and or independent representatives (home-based business owners).

The independent representative helps those newly recruited independent representatives build their own home-based business by helping them identify other customers and independent representatives who desire to own their own home based network marketing business.

Through this duplication and multiplication process, each home-based business owner can recruit and sponsor a few customers and/or independent representatives and, as a result, generate a sizable organization of consumers and marketers.

Referring

Does this sound like a foreign and awkward activity to you?

How many people have you referred to your favorite restaurant, church events, club events, and your favorite movie?

How many more have gone because the people you told enjoyed the restaurant or movie and told someone else who went?

How much did you get paid? We are all already referring customers every day! It is just that most of us don't get paid for it.

The question is not whether we refer customers; the question is whether we are getting paid for the activity!

In network Marketing, customer or independent representatives receive an income for "marketing" the products of the company simply by referring other customers to the company!

Normally, we receive compensation through 10-15 generations and sometimes unlimited of this duplication activity.

In addition, there are usually additional performance, development, and leadership bonus compensation structures! Assuming an association with the right company:

Network Marketing is one of the very few processes I know of where you will earn in relation to your ability and effort with virtually unlimited potential!

Although most people are looking only for a few hundred or few thousand of supplemental monthly income, I personally know, know of, or have met a substantial number of people who earn several tens of thousands of dollars per month from their home-based network marketing business!

Some are even making 7-8 figure income from their home-based network marketing business.

CHAPTER 6

THE MYTHS ABOUT NETWORK MARKETING

Network Marketing has been misunderstood and demonized by many people. It is also regarded by some people as an unimportant or strange business.

But despite the criticisms, myths and false statements about network marketing, network marketing is a viable way to start a part-time home-based business.

The first step to success is to decipher the myths from the truth.

Some of the myths of network marketing are:

Myth # 1: Network Marketing Is an Illegal Pyramid Scheme

In the illegal pyramid test, the shape of an organization does not determine legality. If it did, most businesses and organizations, including the government would be illegal because all have a pyramid structure. An illegal pyramid scheme provides no products or services and pays according to the number of recruits.

Legal network marketing programs offer quality products or services that are sold to consumers. Recruiting new members allows for increased income based on the volume of sales, with team sales volume, not the number of recruits, being the important factor in calculating income.

Other laws legitimate network marketing companies adhere to include publishing average income statistics, no inventory requirements, and refund options.

Myth #2: Only Those at the Top Makes the Most Money

This argument more accurately describes a "job." How often does a minimum wage worker become the Chief Executive Officer (CEO)? Many good employees never get the advancement and financial rewards their quality of work deserves.

This argument suggests that only the people who get in early make money, which isn't true. Many ground-floor distributors make nothing while many who come in years later make a fortune.

The truth is, in good network marketing companies, distributors can make any amount regardless of where they are in the organization. Income is related to effort, not position.

Moreover, while independent distributors of network marketing companies can earn greater income and rewards based on their effort, they don't change position unless people above them leave the organization. That means, no matter when you join or where you are in the organization, you have an equal chance as anyone else to do well if you do the work.

Myth #3: There Is Direct Selling Involve

Network marketing is not about selling products or earning linear income!

The biggest popular misconception about network marketing is that it's a *selling* business. But selling is just earning more income. The problem is if you stop the activity, the income stops.

A salesperson has a job. If you work behind the counter at a department store, you're in the Employee Quadrant; if you're in business for yourself, selling insurance or homes or jewelry, you're in the Self-employed Quadrant. But either way, you have a job, and your job is to sell.

That's not going to build your wealth or your freedom.

What you want is not another job; you want *another address*, one over in the Big Business Quadrant.

People often assume that being successful in this business means being "great at sales." But the point of network marketing is not to become great at selling your particular product or service, because no matter how good you might be at doing that — and let's be honest, if you're like most people, you don't think you *are* very good at it — there's only so much income you can earn selling.

After all, there are so many hours in the day, right?

In network marketing, the whole point is not to *sell a product* but to *build a network*, an army of people who are all representing that same product or service to share with others.

The goal is not for you or any other individual to sell a lot of product; it's for *a lot of people* to be their own best customer, sell and service a reasonable number of customers, and recruit and show a lot of other people how to do the same thing.

And here's the reason you want to build that army of independent representatives: Once you do, you know what you'll have? An asset that generates income for you— *residual* income.

Again, I repeat my statement again: *Network marketing is not about earning more income; it's about building an asset.*

Here's a critical truth about network marketing that may surprise you: It is not a business for those who are gifted in sales.

You know the most successful people in network marketing are not necessarily the best natural salespeople?

For a "born salesman" to succeed in network marketing, often the first thing he or she has to do is *forget everything they know about selling.*

Many of the most successful network marketers I've ever seen have been coaches, mums, pastors teachers — people who really enjoy telling stories and helping others.

Network marketing is about sharing information and personal stories, and not about hard selling. It is also about *caring* about the success of those you bring into the business.

Which is a good thing, by the way, because only one person in twenty is a natural-born salesman anyway.

The key to success in sales is what you can do.

The key to success in network marketing is what you can *duplicate* and it is that duplication factor in network marketing that shows the huge difference between sales and network marketing.

Look, if you are an amazing, uniquely skilled, superstar salesperson, then you can do great in sales—and chances are good, you will do *lousy* in network marketing."

Why? Because while you might sell a lot of products, *most people in your network won't be able to duplicate what you do*. Consequently, your network cannot grow, and it dies an early death.

I've seen it happen many times. I often watch talented and creative people start out in network marketing and run into this brick wall because they think that the way to be successful is to use their ingenuity, talent, and unique skills to be amazing. But it's not a question of what you can do; it's what you can do and then what *others* can do, too.

I have also seen some network marketing companies make the mistake of too strongly recognizing high levels of personal sales as opposed to placing more emphasis on showing everyone how to duplicate their efforts in the performance of others.

The ability to duplicate is the magic key here, not the ability to be a top salesperson. When a network marketing company fails to make this clear, they impair their ability to continuously develop and energize their growth engine: the people who duplicate themselves.

Again, what gives your network marketing business its real power is not what *you* can do; it's what you can *duplicate*. In other words, you want to build your business in a way that virtually anyone else can readily copy. Why? Because others copying what you do is exactly what you want to happen—what you *need* to have happened. That's what creates your success.

Myth #4: Network Marketing Uses People

Many people who complain about network marketing say they don't like the idea of "using" their friends and family to make money.

However, network marketing doesn't reward people for using others. Success in network marketing comes from helping others reach their goals.

A person cannot earn income from the efforts of their recruits without investing time in assisting them to earn income, as well.

Admittedly, some network marketers see potential recruits as dollar signs, but those people are not as successful as those who are genuine in their effort to help their recruits do well.

Myth #5: It Takes Hard Work and Talent to Succeed

Does it take too much hard work, qualification, and talent to succeed in a home-based network marketing business? Absolutely no.

So what does it take to build your own successful network marketing business?

First, let's look at what it *doesn't* take.

1. You don't need an MBA or high-powered business background.

2. You don't have to be "great at sales".

3. You don't need to quit your job!

4. You don't need to be rich or take out a second mortgage on your home.

6. You don't need to be a genius at negotiation or an expert at numbers.

Those are a few of the things it *doesn't* take to build a successful network marketing business.

Now let's look at what it *does* take.

It takes:

1. Being honest with yourself.

2. The right attitude.

3. Commitment.

4. Discipline.

5. Personal Development skills.

Myth #6: Network Marketing Doesn't Work

According to the Direct Selling Association, in 2015 the direct sales industry, of which network marketing is a part of, grossed $36.12 billion in retail sales in the United States. Further, over 20 million people in the U.S. are involved in direct sales.

These numbers indicate that network marketing can work. Success or failure has less to do with network marketing itself, and instead, is determined by the amount effort one puts into their business. Many bloggers, eBayers, Amazon affiliates and other home business owners don't do well or quit too, but you don't hear people saying blogging, or being an affiliate of Amazon and eBay don't work.

Myth #7: Only 3% of Distributors Get Rich in Network Marketing

It's true that not everyone succeeds in network marketing. 2-10% of network marketers earning big money are the same 2-10% who works consistently in their businesses.

But getting rich shouldn't be how network marketing is judged. If getting rich is the measure of success, then many other homes and small business owners, and the majority of employees in traditional jobs are big failures.

Instead, network marketing should be measured by the number of people who reach their goals. Many people in network marketing find success when they earn enough to stay home with the kids or pay off debt and never have to work 9-5. They have control of their time, so they don't trade time for money as employees do.

Myth # 8: In time, the Program Will Get Saturated

Saturation is impossible because there aren't a finite number of people. Every day new people are born or turn 18, thereby adding new potential network marketers to the pool of prospects.

Tim Sales, in Zig Ziglar's book, *Network Marketing for Dummies,* offers the best argument against the saturation myth. He asks, *"Do you know anyone who doesn't have a refrigerator? No? That doesn't stop GE from selling more of them."*

Network marketing like any other business has its issues, but much of them center on false and misleading information. Financial Gurus, such as David Bach and Robert G. Allen both recommend network marketing and direct selling in their books, which suggests that network marketing is gaining some respectability in the mainstream business world.

However, misconceptions and myths persist. Don't let these false beliefs stop you from considering a home-based network marketing business. You can achieve success in a network marketing venture *if you avoid the common network marketing mistakes, gain a solid understanding of the industry, choose a company carefully, find a quality sponsor, and commit time and effort to your business.*

CHAPTER 7

HOW TO CHOOSE A GOOD NETWORK MARKETING COMPANY

Once it has been determined that a home-based network marketing business is appropriate and further determined that a home-based network marketing business is even more appropriate, the real difficulty is in determining which network marketing opportunities to become involved in. Without experience in the industry, unless you're extremely lucky, it is next to impossible to pick a winner on the first try!

Unfortunately, it seems that experience in the industry is not always sufficient for the proper evaluation of a network marketing opportunity. As is the case with traditional business, there are good opportunities and bad opportunities. As is the case with traditional business, unfortunately, many people let their emotions cloud their rational judgment when it comes to evaluating a network marketing company and/or business opportunity!

The Assessment Process

There are certain criteria which must be used rationally when you do an assessment. Consider the following:

1. Competent Company Management Team

Normally it is very difficult for us to know any more about the network marketing company's management team than what they tell us themselves.

The assessment of the management team only becomes an issue with a new company! If a company has been in business three to five years with a well-documented and stable growth record, we really don't need to waste our time.

New network marketing companies are starting up at a higher rate than ever before. It seems that every person who has ever been successful in network marketing wants their own company. Surprise, running a network marketing company is traditional business and new network marketing companies fail at near the same rate as traditional businesses!

2. Age of the Company

The most common mistake made by the masses is getting emotionally tied up in the "ground floor opportunity" pitch which caters to our "greed" and the "fear of loss"! If a person is determined to get involved with a new network marketing company, they should do so because they understand totally the market for the product(s) and the experience of the management team.

Being on the ground floor is usually not best because the majority of new companies will fail. Even if the new company does succeed, there will be many adjustments and changes during the initial growth and there usually is a lack of proven marketing procedures, materials, and training support. The attrition rate is usually much higher during those first years because most individuals are not emotionally flexible enough to accept the changes and turmoil.

A network marketing company experiences four basic phases of growth and market penetration. The risk of the company failing during phase one (usually first 3-5 years) is 10-20 times greater than in phase two. Contrary to popular belief, it usually is far better to be involved with a network marketing company after they're entered phase two.

The risk of their failure is negligible. Their success indicates that their products are acceptable and that their marketing procedures and materials work! Then, either fortunately or unfortunately, our success depends only on ourselves!

3. Little Investment

With the right network marketing opportunity, one should be able to start their own home-based business for hundreds of dollars, rather than the normal thousands, tens of thousands, or hundreds of thousands of dollars usually associated with other traditional businesses which have any serious financial potential!

4. No Inventory, No Receivables, and No Collections

While traditional business owners do an inventory — make or record and report an itemized list of merchandise or supplies on hand, network marketing representatives don't do any inventory, receivable, and collections.

5. No Employees

Employees require a tremendous obligation from the business owner; mentally, emotionally and financially. With network marketing, other independent distributors in our organization, while working their own home-based business, supply the same benefit to us as employees would to a traditional business. We have no payroll, no benefit overhead, no space requirement, and no management duties other than a moral obligation to help others in their business just as others will help us.

6. Residual Income – Persistency

Unless you have been a successful network marketer, insurance agent or marketer, author or actor, it is really difficult to understand the tremendous benefit of residual income.

Starting on a part-time basis, a sincere person or couple with desire and persistence can, within a 3-5 year period, build a meaningful residual income to last a lifetime and then some.

Building a residual income is a little like flying a big jet. It takes a significant amount of fuel to get it off the ground, but once it has reached altitude, it can throttle back and fly on a fraction of the fuel needed for takeoffs.

The big difference is that a residual income can "fly" seemingly forever with a little refueling along the way. The income stream can be passed from generation to generation.

All the other benefits of network Marketing, such as control, opportunity, and flexibility are important, but ***Residual Income is the essence of Network Marketing!***

7. Quality Products

Most network marketing companies have quality products, but many of them lack the 3 essential elements of a good and quality product. Always go for a network marketing company that their products have all the three essential features.

3 Essential Features of a Quality Product

The 3 elements of a good and quality product are:

1. Need: Before you join a network marketing company, consider if there is a need for the products. Are the company's products necessity products? Can a consumer say, "I can't afford, not to have this product?"

2. Consumable: You should partner with a network marketing company if only their products are daily use products and they are not luxurious. Such products can be toothpaste, bathing soap, body cream, sanitary pad, water, and so on. These are things which the poor, the middle class and the rich cannot live without. If your network marketing company produces such products, then you are in business for life.

We all know that everybody bathes, drink water, use cream, and the women always go through their monthly cycle of menstruation unless older. With this in place, you have consumers/customers for life. You will continue to earn more and more money from your consumers/customers for long.

3. Demonstrable: Many network marketing companies have good products with the 2 essential elements discussed above, but lack the third essential element. I'm fortunate to be with a network marketing company that has all these 3 elements.

I love this company for one thing and that is being able to produce products that distributors like me can demonstrate to others and compare them to other similar products in the market, and at the end of the demonstration, my network marketing company's products come out as the winner over other similar products in the market.

8. No Auto-ship

Many and many network marketing companies have this system we call "auto-ship" in place and this makes it hard for many network marketers to excel in this home based network marketing business.

What is Auto-ship?

Auto-ship is whereby a distributor or partner is mandated to personally buy a required volume of products on his own very month to qualify him to earn money on the activities of his downlines or team. In other words,

Auto-ship is also known to be compulsory monthly purchases of products or else sale points wiped away. Without the distributor being able to buy such a required volume of products to earn him the required point value (PV), the company forfeits paying him any money on the activities and efforts of his downlines. Isn't it painful? This is one of the downsides of many network marketing companies.

Again I will say I'm fortunate to be a partner of a network marketing company that has eliminated the auto-ship system from their marketing or compensation plan.

With my company, I'm not mandated to buy products before earning money on the activities and efforts of my downlines.

Experience has taught me that many more people propose to have *desire* and *persistence* than actually *demonstrate* it. The purpose of this book is to identify individuals who sincerely *want* more success in their life but don't seem to have the right *vehicle* for their journey.

If you are one of the few, then I invite you **to join my home-based network marketing business which would allow me to work with you and for you, in order that we both achieve our success goals.** If any of this makes any sense to you and you would like to work with me, send an email to **langmartey@gmail.com** or send a text to **0023 354 500 4563** (it is also my WhatsApp number) and we will get engaged.

To your success,

Anthony Langmartey

"Helping You Achieve Financial Freedom so you can live a better life"

Did you get some value from the information provided in this book? If you did, send me an email and tell me about it.

Connect with Anthony Langmartey

Contact Lines: 0023354 500 4563 or 0023350 491 5960

Email: langmartey@gmail.com

Website: htttps://www.influencernetworker.net

If you wish to join my network marketing team, send me an email.

About the Author

Anthony Langmartey has a degree in Business Administration and specialized in marketing. He is also the founder of thespiritandtruth.com Anthony Langmartey is a deliverance minister, evangelist, author, counselor, public speaker, and network marketer.

Widely known for his work in resolving personal and spiritual conflicts, Anthony maintains brisk counseling, consulting, and speaking schedule.

Anthony also conducts seminars on leadership, wealth, network marketing, marriage, family, biblical prophesies and spiritual identity.

For more info about him and his work visit his business page at **https://www.influencernetworker.net/about-anthony-langmartey/**

Do You Want More Information?

Visit my website for more episodes on how to set up your home-based network marketing business and learn about the skills required to raise your business from the ground to the sky.

Work With Anthony

If you're looking to join my Network Marketing Team and you want to achieve financial freedom and independence then you landed in the right place.

To Find Out How You Can Work Directly With Me Or Join My Network Marketing Team, Click the Button Below:

https://www.influencernetworker.net/applying-for-info/

Another Book By the Author
NETWORK MARKETING SUCCESS BLUEPRINT

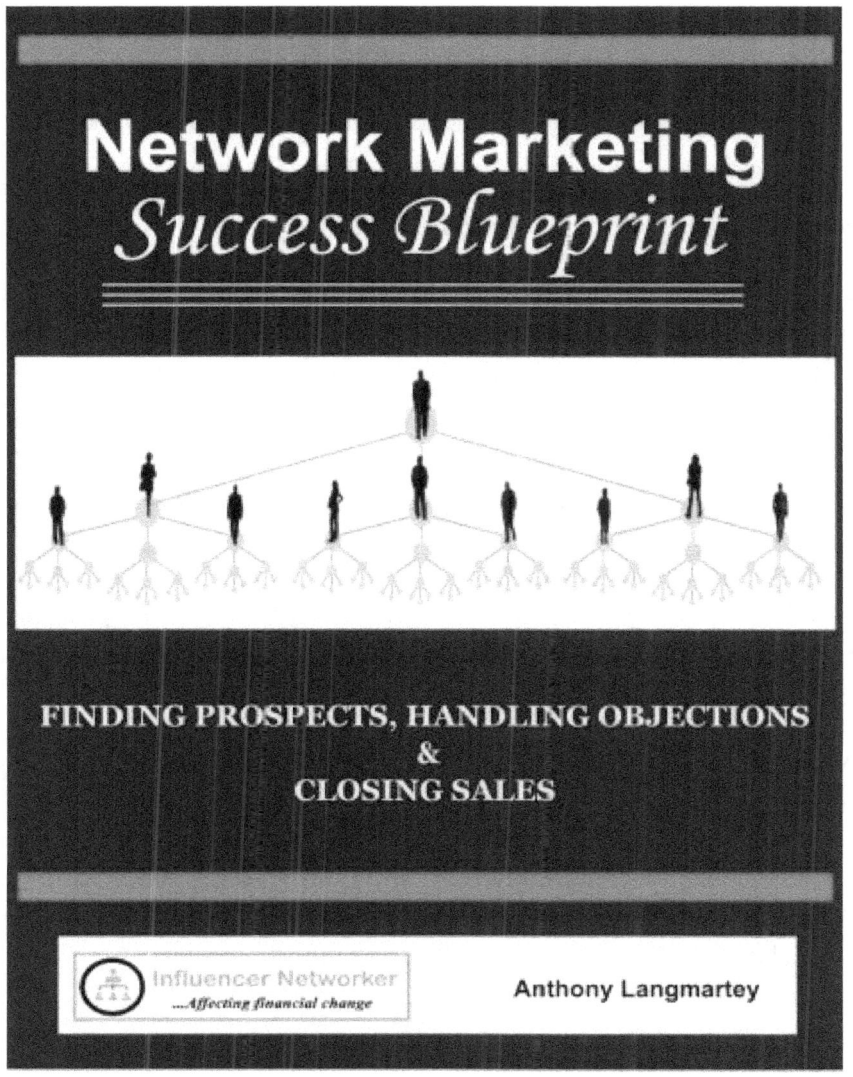

Are you an employee, who wants to start a home business which will not interfere with your job?

Are you a retiree or house mum, who wants to earn extra income from the comfort of your home?

Do you want to have time for yourself to travel around the world, but your current situation or job is not offering you that?

Do you want to escape the rat race and start your own home business?

Are you tired of jumping from one job to another, and wants to earn some extra money without being fired again?

Do you want to build a business empire that can continually generate you unlimited income even though you stop working?

Do you want to create a home business and then will it to whomever you want?

Well, if your answer to any of the above questions is **"YES"**, then this book is written for you.

This book will show you how to solve your financial crises, problems, struggles and create success fast using the internet while designing the lifestyle you love.

Many people are failing in network marketing because they are not doing it right.

Stop wasting your time by doing what is not working and start doing what is actually working and producing high results. It is about time you go professional.

Anthony Langmartey is a professional network marketer and has built a successful business empire with the most profitable downline teams in the last decade.

He has helped his team grow to more than 210, 000 distributors worldwide, including many stories of lives being changed for the better due to the high incomes generated.

How did he arrive at that, he focused on developing his skills and that made him a professional network marketer.

He has poured his years of knowledge, experience, and tactics from working with so many people into the pages of this self-taught book.

In this ultimate blueprint guidebook, you will learn:

✓ **How to find prospects and add them to your name list** (Chapter 2).

✓ **How to use the right invitation script to invite your prospects** (Chapter 3 & 4).

✓ **How to use the right script to handle inviting questions, objections, and excuses of prospects** (Chapter 5).

✓ **How to use the right after invitation follow-up scripts to remind your prospects of the business meeting** (Chapter 6).

✓ **How to meet with your prospects and present the business to them or meet with them at one of your team's business presentation seminars.**

✓ **How to close sales and sign up your prospects** (Chapter 7).

✓ **How to handle the questions, objections, and excuses of your prospects** (Chapter 8).

✓ **How to use the right after business presentation follow-up script to schedule a one on one meeting with your prospects in order to finalize the signup process** (Chapter 9).

And other essential skills you need to develop.

Applying the skills from this book will make you more effective, more profitable, and professional and you will see yourself rising to the top while you are building your network marketing business.

Grab you copy now!

You can get the book from your favorite retailer.

HOW DO I HELP PEOPLE WHO WANT TO START A HOME BUSINESS?

Are you struggling to build your home business or considering starting the Network Marketing profession?[1]

Then you are at the right place and at the right time because I will help you do that simply and easily without any hassle.

You see achieving financial freedom is a goal for many people. Financial freedom generally means having enough savings, investments, and cash on hand to afford the lifestyle we want for ourselves and our families and a growing nest egg that will allow us to retire or pursue the career we want without being driven by earning certain small amounts of money each year. Too many of us fail to reach that goal.

We are burdened with increasing debt, financial emergencies, profligate spending, and other issues that thwart us from reaching our goals. It happens to everyone, but through my books, I will put you on the right path.

I will help you achieve financial freedom and independence if you follow the exact framework and steps I used to go from poverty to financial freedom and independence in less than three (3) years.

I will show you the blueprint to succeed in a home business.

Most importantly, I'll show you how to make enough money so that you never have to work again — unless, of course, you want to.

The more ideas you can implement from me, the faster you will build wealth, change your life, and reach financial freedom. If you want to

---

1. https://www.influencernetworker.net/work-with-anthony/

be able to walk away from the corporate world in less than three years as I did, the surest way to do so is to follow my example step by step. My strategy employs simple techniques, it's **customizable, scalable, and duplicable,** and one you can use indefinitely.

HOW DO I HELP NETWORK MARKETERS?

I also help struggling Network Marketers:

1. Crush It In Business By Creating A Business That Supports A Leveraged And Amazing Lifestyle.

2. Apply Time Tested Processes To Increase Productivity, Maximize Results, And Achieve Success Fast.

3. Expand Their Personal Development And Leadership Skills, Build A Culture And Learn To Create A Thousand Of Themselves And Leading Thousands!

4. Achieve Financial Freedom And Independence By Applying **To Daily Success Practices** Of The Ultra-Rich.

5. Attract Quality Leads.

6. Automate Their Lead Generation And Recruiting To Grow Their Network Marketing Business and Achieve Financial Freedom.

7. Leverage Peak Performance Strategies, Automation & Recruiting Systems, Irrespective Of Existing Experience Or Results.

PS: If you're looking for a way to be mentored as a network marketer or considering coaching, **click here to learn more about my result-driven approach.** [1]

Let me know how I can be of help to you or your business!

Remember to leave me a review.

The Easiest Way to Review My Books

---

1. https://www.influencernetworker.net/my-result-driven-approach/

Step 1: Head Over to your favorite retailer and review the book.

Step 2: Navigate Back to the Book Page

Note: You can also leave a review immediately after you finished purchasing the book by scrolling to the very last page.

Step 3: Scroll down to the "Customer Reviews" section

Click on the "Write a customer review" button

Step 4: Leave a Review and Star Rating

Write your review and click the "Submit" button to complete.

Don't miss out!

Visit the website below and you can sign up to receive emails whenever Anthony Langmartey publishes a new book. There's no charge and no obligation.

https://books2read.com/r/B-A-HOVF-UDTZ

BOOKS 2 READ

Connecting independent readers to independent writers.